CONSCIOUS HOME DESIGN

The Guide to Living Your Best Life by Designing for Happiness, Health, and Relationship Success

TALOR STEWART, ARCHITECT

www.ConsciousHomeDesign.com

Conscious Publishers books may be ordered through booksellers or by contacting:

Conscious Publishers
3233 Sharp Rd.
Glenwood, MD 21738
www.conscious.pub
info@conscious.pub
Conscious Publishers rev. date: 03-24-2019
Print information available on the last page.

The views expressed in this work are solely those of the author and do not necessarily reflect the views of the publisher. The author of this book does not prescribe the use of architecture or home design as a form of treatment or prevention of physical, mental, emotional, or medical problems. Purchase and use of this book do not constitute a client/professional relationship. In the event you use any of the information in this book for yourself, the author and publisher assume no responsibility for your actions. The intent of the author is only to offer information of a general nature to help you in your quest to create a joyful life.

Publisher's Cataloging-In-Publication Data

Names: Stewart, Talor, author.
Title: Conscious home design : the guide to living your best life by designing for happiness, health, and relationship success / Talor Stewart, Architect.
Description: Glenwood, MD : Conscious Publishers, [2019]
Identifiers: ISBN 9781733823401 (softcover) | ISBN 9781733823418 (hardcover) | ISBN 9781733823425 (Kindle) | ISBN 9781733823494 (ePub)
Subjects: LCSH: Interior decoration--Psychological aspects. | Architecture, Domestic--Psychological aspects. | Dwellings--Psychological aspects. | Self-actualization (Psychology) | Feng shui.
Classification: LCC NK2113 .S74 2019 (print) | LCC NK2113 (ebook) | DDC 747.019--dc23

ISBN: 978-1-7338234-3-2 (audio)

Library of Congress Control Number:2019907637

Dedication

This book is dedicated to the Noble New in us all.

Sing songs that none have sung,
Think thoughts that ne'er in brain have rung...

Paramahansa Yogananda

Table of Contents

Preface

There is a paradigm shift happening in home design. Today's marketplace demands more than what the old-world values represent and deliver. Today, new home owners are more design savvy. For the Conscious Homeowner, gone are the days when a house is deemed adequate simply because it is built in X architectural style, has Y number of bedrooms, and Z number of square feet.

Conscious Homeowners expect more from their homes. They want increased functionality, reduced maintenance, and smaller utility bills. They want a home that maximizes their sense of individual freedom and personal privacy, while at the same time fostering greater family connection. They want highly supportive homes that enhance their lifestyle by removing friction and creating ease and grace.

There are different kinds of people in the world. Some are grounded in a pragmatic "What you see is what you get" approach. For these people, the sometimes intangible connection between our external environment and our internal mental, emotional, and spiritual states aren't often considered. For them, little value is placed on these ideas unless they can be empirically proven and demonstrated.

Other people approach life with a more intuitive perspective. They prefer to feel their way through things and trust their gut — sometimes even in the face of what appears to be contrary external evidence. Part of this personal subjectivity is based on bias and preference, but some of it has a ring of universal truth, even if science has yet to prove how or why.

The concepts and principles in this book are for both types of people. Though it is peer reviewed, this book is not an academic paper. It is short, easy to read, and accessible. *Conscious Home Design* is also practical. The principles are applicable to homes of every style and size, whether a 600 square foot cottage or a 60,000 square foot estate.

Architecture is both science and art. Designers keep current with professional research about new building materials, advanced construction techniques, and developments in energy efficiency. Today, it is equally important to incorporate leading edge information from the fields of health, diet, psychology, and neuroscience into design. By integrating many fields of science into a holistic understanding of human needs, innovative architecture can be developed to create homes that actively promote the wellbeing of their inhabitants.

The truth is that from childhood through old age, we spend about half our lives inside our homes. An investment in *Conscious Home Design* is an investment in yourself. It's an investment in your family, your comfort, your values, and your future.

Conscious Home Design is about using architecture to create momentum in the lives of those who experience it. *Conscious Home Design* helps people more readily achieve their noble hopes, dreams, goals, and bright ambitions. *Conscious Home Design* can help us experience more happiness, health, and relationship success.

Introduction

Dear Reader,

If this book caught your eye then we probably share a lot of common ground. We enjoy living a conscious lifestyle; paying attention to the foods we eat, the amount we exercise, and the quality of our sleep. Relationships, both personal and professional, are deeply meaningful. We care about feeling connected; part of the joy, rhythm, and flow of life.

We invest in ourselves, whether in the form of classes, coaches, or trainers in our areas of interest because we value success and enjoy doing the things we do well. We want to grow our knowledge and stay focused and on point to keep moving forward in the direction of our goals and dreams.

When we feel at the top of our game we are indomitable, unstoppable, able to take on the world. On days that feel like an uphill battle a little bit of support and encouragement goes a long way.

We all know the value of close, positive friends and the quality of company we keep. Yet how many people understand the true role and value of smart, conscious design of the homes that keep us?

What if all our best efforts to live consciously through diet, exercise, positive lifestyle and healthy relationships aren't being reinforced — or worse, are being undermined — by the homes we live in? What if our environment is somehow making it harder to achieve our hopes and dreams? All of our best efforts to achieve success and happiness can be hindered by an unsupportive environment.

When we *build* consciously, it becomes easier to *live* consciously. We spend about half of our lives in our homes. Lifestyles vary, but even highly active people spend over one third of their time at home. In the same way that a tree root moves a cement sidewalk by exerting slow but constant pressure over time, the buildings we inhabit also apply a slow and steady pressure on our health and well-being. It is up to us to make sure they guide us in ways that enhance, rather than hinder, our lives.

A Georgetown University study found that student test scores increased by up to 11% simply by improving physical environment. *We can use design to help us excel.* People of all ages, be it kids at school or adults in their offices, can improve productivity with sensitive use of color. *We can use color to help us focus.* Sleep can be deeper and more restful with careful orientation and window placement that optimally times exposure to natural light. *We can use architecture to help us rest and recharge.*

We can apply all these design strategies — and more — to our homes. What would life be like if the design of our homes increased our effectiveness and efficiency, our sense of peace, our feeling of connection and happiness? What doors of opportunity would open to us? Would we walk through our day with an extra spring in our step? How would our interactions with others blossom?

Shifts in environment can create a meaningful difference in our day to day experience, and lead to dramatic results over the long term. *Conscious Home Design* means we are more likely to achieve our goals while also enhancing the journey.

Conscious Home Design encourages individual expression, seeks to strengthen interpersonal connection, and contributes to a beautiful life. By designing around your core values and building in harmony with the rhythms of nature, we can make life more beautiful, more bountiful, and more enjoyable.

Imagine going through life not knowing what size shoes or clothes you wear. The only way you would know how to shop is to put them on and wear them for a bit. The process of trying on and wearing a home isn't as easy. It takes days, weeks and months after being moved in and settled before we start to see the ways in which a home doesn't fit.

Unconscious design can lead to unpleasant and inefficient living conditions. Furniture and other belongings don't quite fit, and that leads to a build-up of clutter and other cleaning challenges. You can have people bumping into each other or a space that is disproportionate to the activity it is supposed to support. Poor design can cause temperature fluctuations or imbalance, high utility and maintenance costs, dark dreary areas, poor air flow, moisture issues, and health problems.

Conscious Home Design, on the other hand, can add to your sense of ease and enjoyment. Things fit. Things flow. Going about your daily activities is smoother, without the feeling that you're struggling through an obstacle course. The home is easier to keep clean, and you save on utility bills and home repair costs.

A well-designed home provides a feeling of personal freedom and also the space to connect — it supports the individual as well as the family.

So let's set ourselves up for success when choosing a home to move into. You do not have to settle for a home that doesn't fit. Even if your home is lovely and works pretty well, upon reading the pages of this book I think you will see little changes you can make to enhance your quality of life by reducing friction, increasing flow, and fostering connection.

The principles of *Conscious Home Design* can be applied to any kind of home, regardless of design size or style; from Colonial to Modern, Craftsman to Contemporary, Cottage to Castle. Rather than being building-centric, or focused on the architecture itself, *Conscious Home Design* focuses on human experience to encourage an individual's personal values and lifestyle goals.

"I want freedom for the full expression of my personality."
- Gandhi

Just as proper diet, exercise, and good relationships are essential components of a happy, successful life, so too is proper home design. When you place the essential parts of life within the context of a consciously designed home, you and your loved ones will be served and supported day and night.

Whether you rent, own, or build new, you will find something in these pages to help make the place you call home sweeter, more personal, more conscious. Once you *know*, you will never see architecture the same way, and you'll be glad you have this understanding and new way of seeing home design.

CONSCIOUS HOME DESIGN

for Happiness, Health, and Relationship Success

Chapter 1

What's the Big Idea?

Better Living Through Conscious Design

Here's the Big Idea in 177 words: Conscious Home Design *helps us live happier, healthier, more fulfilling lives. Essentially, good design is good for us.* Conscious Home Design *helps us — from our most basic immediate physiological need for oxygen, to the subtler emotional need of feeling a loving connection.*

Supportive environment gives us a lift and makes life easier. A well-designed, beautiful space helps us lead happy, healthy lives. Unsupportive environment, on the other hand, makes us feel constricted, hampered. We can all recognize the stifling effects of poor environment and instinctively avoid them. While neutral environment doesn't hinder us, neither is it particularly encouraging, and we can design better than that.

Clearly, environment shapes us in ways subtle and overt, for good or ill. The highest aim of Conscious Home Design *therefore is to create spaces to ensure that not only the physical, but our mental, emotional, and spiritual needs are met too. When our physical needs are met we survive.* Conscious Home Design *creates greater opportunity to pursue our long-term needs and goals - the things that help us truly thrive.*

This idea is something we understand intuitively. We all know that we need more than food and shelter to satisfy our complex natures. We have mental, emotional, and spiritual aspects to us that need to be expressed and fulfilled.

The scope of human needs has been articulately outlined by the famous psychologist Abraham Maslow. In the 75 years since he first published this hierarchy of needs it has been used in multiple fields and countless scenarios. To design homes that create opportunity for achievement in all areas of human experience, it is helpful to reference Maslow's hierarchy of human needs to show what "happier and healthier" really means so we can use design to achieve it.

At the bottom, we have our most basic and immediate physiological needs. It doesn't do a person much good to feel that they are respected if at the same time they are freezing or on the edge of starvation. We must have our physical needs met before we can begin to fulfill our "higher" needs.

Conventional architecture concerns itself chiefly with the physical by providing safe access to shelter for sleeping, bathing, food preparation, etc. We have extensive laws to safeguard the public around the physical structures they inhabit. Our building and zoning codes ensure that dwellings meet our basic physical requirements. The assumption of these regulations is that if people have a roof that doesn't leak, a front door that locks, and hot and cold running water then it's up to them to go ahead and pursue the American dream.

Traditional homes allow for family interaction in spaces such as a dining room or living room. These spaces suggest some attention to our love and belonging needs, however, our full social, emotional and self-fulfillment needs are often overlooked and forgotten in design. These areas are typically left to individuals to create for themselves, while building codes exist primarily to ensure minimum safety and physical requirements.

Through *Conscious Home Design* we engage design elements that meet our full range of human needs, thereby supporting a fulfilling life. By building intentionally we eliminate some of the friction and inertia that can get in our way. Moving through a Consciously Designed Home guides us more easily and gracefully, making fulfillment of our higher needs easier to experience.

Because most homes already meet basic physical needs, even subtle design changes can yield powerful results. This is nicely illustrated by the Butterfly Effect, which suggests that the flap of a butterfly's wings in Brazil can eventually set off a tornado in Texas. Big results are generated through *sensitive dependence on initial conditions.* Like a snowball effect, slight shifts in initial conditions lead to significant differences later when they are added to and compounded over time.

Another way we can illustrate the great effects of small beginnings is to think of an IRA or 401(k) retirement account. If we take $100,000 and put it in our account and let it grow for 30 years at 5% interest, it turns into a little over $432,000 even if we never add another nickel. By the power of compounding interest alone the money has more than quadrupled — awesome!

However, if you were able to let that same hundred thousand dollars grow at 7% interest instead of 5% for the same 30-year period, you'd end up with over $760,000! That tiny 2% difference leads to a whopping 76% increase in results — for many people the $328,000 difference those 2 percentage points yield have life-changing ramifications.

As with the IRA, what would happen if we arranged things so that people were experiencing just 2% less friction on a day-to-day basis? Knowing how those two little percentage points lead to dramatic life-changing cumulative results, what would it look like not only to feel less friction and stress, but also to experience more grace and ease?

Throughout the design of the home, we're going to look for ways to soften and reduce friction points and increase ease and grace. In the introduction we noted the short-term Georgetown study that showed architectural environment alone was responsible for an 11% increase in test scores. Over a longer period of time, even two percentage points lead to big results. And by designing our homes to gain multiple 2% shifts in various ways, they add up to immediate tangible results in our short-term experience as well.

In art, we say that every stroke of the brush changes the whole composition. The philosopher Johann Gottlieb Fichte wrote that a single grain of sand cannot be moved without changing something throughout the immeasurable whole. These are different ways to describe the interdependence of all things, and how small or seemingly disconnected parts are actually an influential part of the whole.

I had a personal experience that exemplifies this truth. After high school I paused my academic pursuits and started a little company building drums inspired by the west African traditions. I sold the drums out of the workshop and at shows and festivals, and I supplied about 65 wholesale accounts, including Sam Ash music stores. I then sold the business and did some traveling before going to college to study architecture.

During my travels (I've been to 49 states so far) I was invited to a party where I was told there would be plenty of fun drumming. I decided to go, but arrived late with no drum in hand. When I opened the front door, I saw about twenty people in a circle in the living room, pounding away. The party was well under way and all the drums were taken, except one: a tiny little toy of a drum about six inches tall with a head so small I could only play it with my two index fingers. I laughed, realizing that I wouldn't even be able to hear myself let alone have anyone else hear it. What music would I really be contributing to the circle? But I wanted to play so I sat down and got busy with this tiny drum.

The rhythm in the room was pretty free-flowing. I had drumming skills from years of playing for dance classes and other events, but most of the people here were inexperienced and just having fun. There is a great saying from Africa — *if you can walk, you can dance, if you can talk, you can sing.* It means we all have music inside and we can all express it regardless of how much we've practiced. And the folks at this party were doing just that. This wasn't any recognizable, traditional composition or rhythm, it was just gyrating, pulsating organic thunder.

At some point it began to feel stagnant, directionless, faltering, like it had lost its path. So I used my intention to lead the way. On the little toy drum, I played the rhythm and tempo I felt the circle needed; lo and behold the whole circle followed. Now, maybe that was a coincidence. Maybe I was just part of the flow. No one could hear me; I couldn't even hear my own drum. So I tried it again, deliberately changing the rhythm again. The circle followed again. A third time: same thing. I realized this was no coincidence, this was *influence*.

Then, I let go, and just played. Sometime later when the circle finally slowed and came to a rest, I felt a profound serenity and expansiveness. While others began to chat and start up conversations, I reflected silently.

I received a great lesson that evening. Even though I can't fully explain the mechanics behind it, I learned that every tap of the drum affects the whole, no matter how small or quiet or seemingly insignificant. So play your song! Even if it's just for yourself. Especially if it's just for yourself. Leave the results up to nature and enjoy the moment.

In *Conscious Home Design* we look for ways to customize a design and layout around your family's lifestyle goals and individual personalities so you can better sing your song. With this metaphor, we can think of the home as an "instrument" for living. When we look for and make multiple little shifts from room to room in a home we "tune" it to your choosing and make a sort of music of your life.

So let's take a look at some of the ways that we can make positive changes beginning with our most basic human needs of food, water, and air.

Physiological Needs
Using Scientific First Principles to Prioritize Home Design

We all need clean air to breathe, wholesome food to eat, and fresh water to drink. The Rule of Sevens says that the strongest, healthiest people can go up to seven weeks without food, seven days without water, and seven minutes without air. For the average person, that number is around three.

Air, water, and food are very immediate physiological needs, and even a small increase in quality and purity affects both our short- and long-term health and enjoyment. Because life is so fundamentally influenced by these essential needs it makes sense to prioritize them in *Conscious Home Design* and expand from there.

Sharing delicious food is a wonderful way to come together with friends and family. The social aspect of eating is enjoyed by people and cultures all over the world. Besides social pleasures, food provides our bodies with essential fuel. The body-mind connection is enhanced by excellent nutrition. Our physical and mental performance benefit from a consistently healthy diet. In the chapters on kitchen and dining we will take a closer look at how we can use *Conscious Home Design* to enhance our social enjoyment and nutritious benefit from eating and preparing food.

We also want to make sure our homes have plenty of good clean water. While individual water intake needs vary based on lifestyle and body size, we all need to stay hydrated. I was alarmed when I read that The Institute of Medicine reported that as many as 75% of Americans suffer from chronic dehydration— a condition that yields increasingly devastating health results the longer it persists.

The truth is, no one wants to drink stale-tasting water that smells like chlorine every day. Even if the water that comes out of the tap is considered safe and potable by EPA standards, that doesn't mean that it's actually going to *taste* good. There's a difference between not being harmful and being actively beneficial and adding vitality into our lives.

Let's take a moment to recognize that delicious-tasting water is essential for people to drink enough to maintain proper hydration. Clean, fresh water is not only delicious, it is energizing, rejuvenating, and revitalizing. We'll cover some design features we can use to encourage hydration in the kitchen and bathroom sections.

Have you ever found yourself experiencing an ocean breeze at the oxygen-rich seashore, or perhaps in the high crisp mountain air enjoying a big deep breath and smiling at the invigorating feeling it gives? In *Conscious Home Design* we explore design strategies that place indoor air quality as the highest priority.

Because we spend so much time in the home, fresh vital air is especially important to have. We want more than air that simply isn't toxic. What we really want to breathe is air that is charged with vitality and freshness and energy so that it actually gives us a little lift.

When the air is fresh we enjoy being inside more and it nourishes us. Stuffy, musty, stale air has the opposite effect and leads to feeling groggy and sluggish. Air that is too humid leads to mold and mildew. Clothes get musty, and towels take longer to dry and get a funky smell more quickly. Excessively dry air leads to dry respiratory passages vulnerable to dust and illness. Dry air also increases uncomfortable static electricity.

Even though air quality is so crucial, traditional architecture frequently undervalues this fundamental reality. While we all know that air is the single most important thing for our immediate survival, the practice of using chemicals in common building materials and sealing every door, window, and crack for energy efficiency leads to poor indoor air quality.

Many homes have poorer air quality than the air outside. It is so common and widespread that industry experts have named it Sick Building Syndrome. Houses built in the construction boom after WWII we began using more chemicals in glues and paints and other construction materials.

Over the next few decades builders became more efficient at tightening and sealing up the building envelope so that we had less outside air exchange and circulation. Though building codes and the laws regulating manufacturing have made progress since then, we can still do better.

NASA did an extensive clean air study for the benefit of their astronauts. They tested dozens of plants to see which ones produced more oxygen and were most effective at filtering the air of gasses and toxins like ammonia, benzene, and formaldehyde – common in many household supplies, building materials, and cleaning products. Some of the most effective plants are *Gerber Daisy, Dracaena Marginata,* and *Bamboo Palm. Peace Lily* and *Florist's Chrysanthemum* also showed significant air-cleaning properties. We can learn from this, and for household or office use it is recommended to have at least one plant per 100 square feet.

Air quality is key throughout the whole home, but it plays an especially important part in bedrooms because we spend so much time there. Our breathing is generally shallower during sleep, so it is helpful to have pure, fresh, vital, oxygen-rich air to help us sleep more deeply and wake up feeling refreshed and recharged. As we go through the different room chapters detailing the nine essential spaces we will look at air quality more.

<u>Safety and Security Needs</u>
Being Warm, Dry, and Safe

The next level on the hierarchy of needs pyramid is safety needs: Security and Safety. We can use design to protect ourselves, our homes, and our valuables from fire, flood, storms, theft, and intrusion — whether human or animals and insects.

Conscious Home Design means taking a careful look at the unique circumstances of the building location and the needs of the homeowner. A homeowner in Texas or Oklahoma may desire a tornado shelter for peace of mind. A celebrity or public-facing homeowner might want a hidden safe-room to retreat to while security and law enforcement arrive in the event of intrusion. And every home should have a water and fireproof safe to store passports, jewelry, hard drive backups and other essentials in case of misfortune.

In addition to providing a sense of safety for ourselves and security for our possessions, we want to protect the home itself. My clients have saved thousands of dollars in insurance premiums and enjoyed lower deductibles on their policies because of careful design and selection of roofing, siding, and other materials which are rated for resistance to hail, wind, fire, and other hazards. *Conscious Home Design* can save money.

Home security also encompasses more than the house structure. How the building sits on the land, and how the landscape is designed, illuminated, and managed are factors in reducing the likelihood of flood, fire, and storm damage as well as intrusion and vandalism. During my work on housing projects in the public and private sectors I have seen firsthand the role the exterior environment plays in property and personal safety and security.

As a designer and creator, I tend to be optimistic and believe we are better off when we focus on our goals rather than our fears. As Thoreau said, *Go confidently in the direction of your dreams.* However, as a pragmatic and analytical thinker, I also look for ways to limit risk and make it easier for homeowners to relax and focus on those dreams. When it comes down to it, most people want to relax and enjoy being at home with their friends and family. It's what life is all about.

Love and Connection
Experiencing the Joy of Connecting and Feeling of Belonging

We build safe and sturdy homes that provide us a place to rest and bathe and eat and breathe so that we can get on with what we actually want to do with our lives. Once we establish a solid foundation and a safe, healthy environment in our homes, we can use design to foster stronger relationships with those around us.

Connection, belonging, loving and being loved — these are experiences that make life fuller and richer. Understanding different types of relationships means we can design and provide nurturing spaces throughout a home to encourage them in their various forms.

We have relationships where we receive more than we give, such as those we have with our elders, ancestors, mentors, heroes, inspirational and spiritual figures. We have relationships where the giving and receiving are balanced, as we do with our friends, colleagues, neighbors and peers. We also have relationships with those to whom we give more than we receive, such as with students or those we mentor. This includes those we nurture such as children, plants, and pets, or others that we have a responsibility to care and provide for.

Of course, we often also receive in some way from the relationships where we are the primary giver, so in the end there can be an unexpected balance. On the surface however, all of our relationships appear to be in one of the three basic exchange categories: Equal, Giving, or Receiving.

In *Conscious Home Design* we seek to create opportunity within the home to experience all three kinds of relationships. Different people, personalities, and phases in life will vary the amount of each type we experience, but we can use design to allow us the richness and reward of all three kinds on a daily basis.

Even if you live alone, a home can provide for all three relationships. We can be equals when a living area provides chairs or space for more than one, giving us a chance for interaction with guests. A sunny window can offer a place for a houseplant or two, which allows us a giving relationship (and the benefit of fresher air as we learned from NASA) and we can find a prominent place to hang a picture of a parent, teacher, or spiritual figure to remind us of the support and care we receive from others.

We can take this a step further and surround ourselves with the richness of connection by providing space for each relationship type in *every* room. Even bathrooms, which we typically think of as no more than a utilitarian space to care for the body, can accommodate all three relationships. We can easily create a niche for a picture or icon to remind us of those who give to us, and provide enough light for a little plant or even a fishbowl or aquarium. We can build an oversized tub for two if that appeals, or have twin sinks to brush teeth side-by-side with someone.

With thoughtful design, we can plan and build relationship spaces into our homes to help us feel deep and well-rounded connection in our daily lives. *As we go through the nine essential spaces chapters, we will look closely at more specific ways to create both the connection and privacy that healthy relationships require within a consciously designed home.*

We take care to design intentionally for relationships because after our basic physical needs are met, having good relationships is the single biggest predictor of happiness and health. The Harvard Study of Adult Development recently reported this after tallying the data from a study that started over 75 years ago. This study, the most comprehensive and longest on happiness in history, found that education, career success (or failure) and affluent or poor upbringing played less of a factor in how happy, healthy, and long lived a person was than the quality of their relationships.

Because of the mind-body connection, a sense of mental and emotional well-being really influences our physical well-being. True, there are examples of people who are healthy and happy and come down with an inexplicable illness, but in general it's fair to say that happier people tend to be longer-living people. *Strong personal relationships and social integration are the strongest predictors of health and happiness.* Being loved, and loving others is good for us. And when tough times do come, these relationships help us through them. So let's design our homes for relationship success, and the health and happiness that comes with it.

Esteem Needs
Designing without to foster self-esteem within

It feels good to feel good about ourselves! When we are proud of an accomplishment or ability it gives us the boost and confidence to go forward and reach for more of what we want and love in life. Imagine experiencing that feeling of accomplishment every day. Would that put a spring in your step?

We can design homes to do two things for us: First, we can create little reminders and reinforcements in our homes to show us our success and keep our achievements close at hand and at the top of our minds. Second, we can design our homes in ways that actually strengthen the areas in which we are working to excel, thereby increasing the likeliness of success. This, in turn, reinforces our achievement-and-esteem loop.

For instance, if you have felt a sense of accomplishment about running a half marathon, and have a goal of running a full one, we can incorporate both proof of your past victory and supportive elements to keep you on point with your training. As the space celebrates your past and encourages your future, it empowers you in the current moment. Then, when you ultimately meet with success in your latest endeavor, it further adds to your sense of accomplishment and personal esteem.

This strategy can be applied in all areas of your home, whether to encourage physical activity, food and diet routine, relationship goals, creative expression, study and personal development or meditation. The more we live by our values the better we feel about ourselves. When we reach our worthy ambitions in any area it gives us more momentum, creating a springboard to help us in other parts of life.

Self-Actualization
Achieving full potential and creative activities

Self-actualization. Creative expression. Pursuing our genius. Developing our talents and living our passions. These are what turn a good life into a great one. We can have a rich life with good food, relationships, satisfying work, and various activities and entertainment to choose from — but when we find and add a meaningful way to express our inner passion, vision, and creativity, we can say life has truly become great.

When we connect with our personal genius and are able to express our talents for others to experience it gives us a deeper sense of purpose beyond our mundane duties and enjoyments. It gives us (another) reason to get up in the morning. We sometimes hear this referred to as "knowing your why" and it gives us the strength and determination to overcome challenges and successfully navigate the ups and downs of life.

The Japanese call this sense of life purpose "ikigai" and it is a cornerstone of personal fulfillment. As with relationships, having a deep and meaningful sense of purpose is a strong predictor of a person's health, happiness, and longevity.

We are infinitely more likely to experience this self-actualized state when we create space within our homes for passion, creative expression, study, and growth. In the same way we prepare a new room for a soon-to-be-born baby, we also have to create and prepare space for our creative "brain children."

These creative ideas, impulses, and other aspects of our inner selves need care and nurturing to be born and brought to life. Our homes can support us in this way. This is *Conscious Home Design*.

The Sunny Window Effect
The Warmth and Welcome of a Ray of Sunlight

Have you ever walked by a room with beams of sunlight streaming in and noticed how inviting it was? Perhaps sunlight was shining on a comfortable bed or sofa, or even just a bright sunny patch on the floor? Cats waste no time finding these spaces to occupy, and we, too, are naturally drawn to them.

We can use this "sunny window effect" to support us in any area or activity of our home depending on which needs and goals we want to enhance. When the sun is shining into a space we feel drawn in, it's much more attractive than when the sun is hidden behind clouds or curtains. Even an already beautiful room is more appealing when the sun shines in.

Knowing this sunny window effect is a universal experience, think about the activities you would like to encourage and support. If, for example, you want to make sure to keep on top of your reading list, placing a reading room or study in a location of the home that gets direct sun exposure can give a little support and encouragement. A nice sunny reading nook is a good place to spend some time each day, or a couple of hours each week if that is all the time you can manage.

We can use this sunny window effect and our natural response to it to help us reach our goals, and also to aid in doing things that are essential to running the bigger picture of our lives, even though we might not especially enjoy these activities. It is not hard to image how setting ourselves up in a sunny window can make paying bills, folding laundry, or changing diapers a little more pleasant. We will explore more opportunities to apply the sunny window effect as we go through the essential spaces chapters.

Chapter 2

The Nine Essential Activity Spaces

How Zones Help Us by Degrees of Connection

Living a full, rich, well-rounded life means caring for both our physical and non-physical natures. An ideal home creates space for us to express our natures and meet the full range of needs outlined in the pyramid. Though we choose from a nearly infinite variety of activities based on our individual inclinations, they all fit into some element of the needs pyramid. From the wide variety of activities, we can condense them down to a list that can typically be well served by a few rooms.

The ideal home, the Consciously Designed Home, supports 9 key activities: The Entry Hall or Foyer for arriving and departing; the Living room for family connection; the Kitchen for food preparation, The Dining room for eating together or peacefully on our own; the Bedroom for sleeping, vulnerability and intimacy; the Bathroom for care of the body; a Movement space for outer physical development; a Study or Meditation room for inner personal development; and a Creative space for expressing our inner thoughts and feelings to the outside world.

Of course a functional and practical home will also have ancillary spaces: closets and storage, a garage, equipment or tool shed, and utility spaces for water heating and other mechanical needs, and so on. These secondary areas are purely support features and built as needed to serve the functions of the primary activity spaces. Though essential, for our homes, they do not represent Maslow's human activity needs directly.

Sometimes needs and spaces blend. For instance, a dancer and choreographer would have physical movement and creative spaces that are one and the same. Though movement is primarily a physiological need, becoming adept or accomplished in a type of creative or physical movement can also support our esteem needs. Physical activity can serve to support more than just physical health (and the mental health those good endorphins release). We are much more likely to maintain a physical activity if it also satisfies a creative, esteem, or other need. We can thereby transform something that can feel like a chore into a fun activity. Fun is also an essential human need!

Many people find their creative or physical activities outside the home at a class or studio, or on a nearby jogging trail. If a home has immediate access to nature or a studio the world around becomes the activity space. Being outside or in a group can be more fun and help motivate us. Oftentimes being in a class or working with a coach or trainer we push harder than we might on our own.

A home gym or creative space is not meant to replace outdoor time or classes if we enjoy them. It is simply smart to include spaces for these activities within the home for our long-term benefit. There will be days when the weather or time constraints or health challenges limit our ability to partake in activities outside the home. Having a sanctuary within our home for all our needs is planning for success. We do this in addition to our outdoor and away-from-home activities. If your preferred activity is distance cycling or skiing or playing a team sport we can still create space at home that supports that. We'll cover this as we go through the individual rooms in the following chapters.

Spaces need to be dedicated to their activity. In addition to including space for all our needs categories, a thoughtful arrangement and layout that allows for separation of different activities is helpful. We support our efforts in each activity when we compartmentalize our spaces for several reasons. Bedrooms and bathrooms typically require a higher degree of privacy than a living room or kitchen. Some spaces need to be isolated because of sound or dust or odor, such as in a music room or art studio.

Another reason for separation between spaces is that many activities have accoutrements and paraphernalia unique to them, such as pottery wheel, sewing machine, standing computer desk, weights, or exercise equipment.

These activity-specific items need to be set up and left in place, or easily accessible if they can be tucked away but with enough open space to use them when brought out. It is clumsy to have to put away the items from an art project to clear a space to do some yoga or stretching, or have to fold the bed back up to a couch every morning to turn the bedroom into a living room.

A third reason for separate spaces is that some activities take longer than one session to complete. Art work, models, train sets, and musical compositions are some examples of work that can take time. When we can spread out and step back to view and reflect (sometimes for hours or days) before returning with fresh inspiration, we do better work with more flow. It is precisely because of architecture and the ability to create dedicated spaces isolated from the weather and other activities that such progress has been made in art, science, and technology.

The longer we dedicate a room to a particular focus or activity the more "tuned" it becomes. It is as if the space becomes "charged" with the mental intention or emotional frequency associated with the activity or person engaging in it. Have you ever entered a bedroom (yours or someone else's) and suddenly felt tired or drowsy? The energy there may be sleepy, hushed and lulled, and if we are in a receptive mood we can pick up on it. If we pause to notice, we will find this type of experience is common.

Part of this experience is caused by autosuggestion; if we associate a space with an activity then we may subconsciously prepare ourselves for that experience when we see something that triggers it — like having our mouth water upon seeing a refrigerator, even if we aren't especially hungry. Beyond this however, there is a sort of energy build-up from prolonged and repeated intention and activity that stays in a space like a battery storing up energy when plugged into a power source. We are a kind of power source; our willpower and focus serve to charge or fill up empty space like a battery or well.

Whether from autosuggestion or the tendency of a room to hold an energetic charge, the effect is desirable — something we can use to our advantage. The stronger the charge or suggestion is, the more it influences us when we're there. This means that our creative spaces become more creative, and actually encourage us to get into creative flow when we enter. We may not feel particularly like studying, or meditating, or exercising, but when we enter a well-charged library or meditation room or home gym the space gives us a little lift and helps get us in the mood. We create a positive feedback loop.

Having clarified the top reasons for separation, let's briefly look at degrees of isolation. While certain spaces require partition, some areas can be separate but joined. A bedroom or bathroom typically requires the ability to be completely enclosed, however common spaces such as kitchen, dining, and family rooms, while separated, can also be open to each other to facilitate connection and interaction among family members and house guests. When spaces are complementary they serve us better by being adjoined.

Creating separate rooms and spaces for our activities does not necessarily mean having a huge home. We can comfortably apply the design principles of *Conscious Home Design* to cottages as small as 600 square feet that accommodate a single person or a couple with complimentary lifestyles, and scale up from there to suit a large family with many diverse activities. Your personal tastes, needs, finances, and lifestyle will determine the best size for your home.

Finally, spaces can be repurposed and used for a different activity as we need. They are adaptable, so just because it was used as a bedroom in one phase doesn't mean that it can't be turned into a study or an exercise room at a later date. The location of a space still matters with regard to overall layout and flow, but in general space is versatile.

Unless there are major architectural design elements or some very deeply entrenched history to a space, the process of removing furniture, repainting, opening windows to get new air, and moving in new appointments is typically enough to "reboot" a space. This is good news for us as we adapt and shift our lifestyles and interests, or put a home on the market to benefit a new owner with different needs. *Conscious Home Design* plans for an active life. As our lives evolve, our homes evolve with us.

Chapter 3

The Heart of the Home

Building a Home Around What You Love

Why do we build our homes? Why do we work so hard to provide a good home for ourselves and our loved ones? Our homes are the hub around which our lives revolve. A career-driven individual may feel that life revolves around their work, with the home being a satellite of this endeavor that serves to support them in performing their vocation. But at the end of the day, beyond our need for shelter, it comes down to having and providing space for what we love. For most people that means spending time with family and friends — being together.

The living room is a place to tell the story of your family. It's a place where families come together, by the fireplace or around a comfortable seating area. It's a place of tradition, where stories are told, history is passed down from one generation to the next; important knowledge that gives us continuity. It's also a place where little daily details and interactions with each other can happen; little things that are the glue that keep us connected.

Here is where you celebrate what you hold dear in life. Everything else in the home supports this. The core of the home is served by the other spaces. Bedrooms and bathrooms for rest and washing, kitchen and dining for eating, all these functions allow us to live more fully and richly in our interactions with others. The living room is about creating a space that allows people to be together actively (as in participating in a group activity) or passively (like being together but each doing separate things).

The living room is a place where family can be together by simply *being* together, whereas in the kitchen and dining and other areas of the home family time is typically defined by a specific activity. This distinction is why the living room is the true heart of the home and not the kitchen as is sometimes said. It's true that life revolves around food, and often the loving person or people who prepare it, but if we look more closely, we will see that the food is a supportive element and the love of our family members is what living together is really about.

The living room is a community space, and because of this communal nature it makes sense to design this space to be a collage, a collective of everyone's tastes and styles. If the living room only suits the preferences of one person, then it's great for them but not so great for others. The living room is really a collective spatial representation of everybody in your household. It needs to tell everyone's story — the family as a whole *and* as individuals.

When we design like this we nurture a sense of connection. If everyone feels that they belong and is comfortable in the space, then it's going to help our relationships and family dynamic. By using smart design in this simple way, family time can be much more satisfying. Does this make sense? The living room is the heart of the home. It is really the reason we have homes. Without a personal feeling of connection, a house is just shelter. Even if they live alone, a person can create connection with decor, space for guests, and things that remind them of what's meaningful.

How do you want to connect with your friends and family? What values and stories do you want to tell in your home? One person's core values might be fun, family, and freedom. Another person may cherish law, order, and security. There is a way to express these ideals through design and decoration.

As a designer with a goal to create spaces that help everyone experience fuller, richer, more self-actualized lives, I developed a unique discovery process to understand the needs and desires of each member of a household, and generate a palette of elements to inform their design.

Once the palette is created, it can be used to evaluate design choices in our living environment, whether you're building a brand new custom home, or just redecorating your existing one. It can also be used when shopping for a pre-existing home or apartment to help evaluate properties and select one that is a great match. You can learn more about the discovery process at ConsciousHomeDesign.com

It's a fun and thoughtful exploration into the qualities that make you unique, and how to design and build around them to create a space that feels comfortable while also supporting your good habits and lifestyle goals.

Chapter 4

Dining Together

"We come together for dinner to be a family."
Grandpa

What does your ideal mealtime look like? Is it quiet and contemplative or is it animated and boisterous? Is your table surrounded with family and friends telling stories of the day, updating each other and telling jokes in lively conversation with lots of laughs and celebration? Or is it just you and one or two other close and dear ones speaking with soft voices by candlelight, and maybe some low volume music for atmosphere?

A dining room can be these and more, depending on whom we eat with and when. The tone of breakfast can be different from dinner. Friday dinner might be different from Sunday dinner. Meals can vary in tone from one sitting to the next, one day to the next, one season or holiday to the next.

However we come together, the purpose is the same — to enjoy food and company. Even if we live alone we can have a spare chair for a guest. The decorations, furniture, even dishes can all be reminders of family history, or family goals and how we like to live.

How does our dining room allow for the varied ways we use it? Is it inward facing, with the focus of the meal the centerpiece of the table and the people seated around it? Or does it expand, looking towards a view of nature or piece of art that all can appreciate together during mealtime?

On the human needs pyramid, the dining room satisfies our physiological needs for food, and supports love and belonging. The dining room can also expand to meet esteem needs. Raising a beautiful family is an admirable accomplishment. A well-made meal can be a source of pride — in some families it's even something to brag about! A dining room can be a kind of affirmation, a statement of our values and life goals. We can create a space that reflects who we are, and who we might become as we grow.

For example, a view of nature from a picture window in the dining room can be a reminder of enthusiasm for outdoor sport, activity, or conservation if those are strong family values. A painting or relief mural can depict a scene that represents our family's future goals or affirms past history — pride in who we were and who we've become. In these ways we can explore design features that expand into the self-actualization region of the pyramid.

So some of these concepts are grander, big picture ideas that use subtlety and metaphor to reinforce our complex natures. On a more basic practical level, the dining room is a place where we can take in a meal together more slowly instead of rushing through meals to get somewhere — out the door, or to watch a TV show. A kitchen table or island where we sit on barstools is much more a "grab a quick snack and go" experience.

This is okay some of the time, but is counterproductive to family connection as a lifestyle. When we create a dedicated room specifically for the family to come together, it encourages us to take a breath and enjoy ourselves. The dining room supports us with a focus on eating and being present. This helps us slow down, have some peace, and be together as a family, helping create and maintain a strong family bond.

Whether it's breakfast, lunch, or dinner, when the family comes together for a meal, it's a time to touch base with each other, see how things are going, enjoy some good food and replenish ourselves.

Like the communal design of the living room, we want to select architectural features, colors, furnishings and design elements that appeal to everyone in the family. When people feel comfortable in the dining area, interactions (and appetite) are more likely to be fulfilling, harmonious, and happy.

Chapter 5

Preparing Food - The Kitchen is the Cornerstone of a Healthy Family

"Breakfast is the most important meal of the day!"
Grandma

A dining room's full potential isn't realized without a good kitchen! A kitchen's purpose is to help us prepare great food that is good for us - and it should allow us to do that with ease. It's where we ensure the food and water we give ourselves is pure, delicious, nutritious, and prepared with love and care. The more ease and grace our kitchens allow us, the more we will enjoy making good, fresh, nourishing food.

Magazines and blog articles are filled with pictures of showcase kitchens with beautiful cabinets and counters, state-of-the-art appliances, and interesting lighting and decor. These design features do little for the efficiency and convenience of preparing a meal, however.

When the kitchen is set up inefficiently it takes more time and energy to prepare a meal that's good and healthy. That little environmental challenge subtly inclines us to prepare food that's not as well-rounded with fewer ingredients, or perhaps opt for something pre-packaged (i.e. not as fresh and nutritious) that we can grab easily.

Over time this kind of diet will have an impact on our nutrition, and our energy and vitality levels will fade. Our food satisfaction level will drop as well, because nothing is as good as fresh, vitally charged food. If we cut little corners in these areas and our food satisfaction goes down at home, then we will be inclined to eat out more often; if we aren't happy with the variety and nutritional quality of our food at home, we will look elsewhere.

When we eat out, we have less control of what we eat — the chef chooses their recipes which may not be well-balanced, or may contain excess fats, sugars, and carbs or whatever ingredients we may wish to limit or avoid. Restaurant food is typically immediately satisfying and rewarding to the taste buds but not necessarily in our best interest to eat for our overall nutritional health and well-being — especially when we eat it more frequently.

Food is as good for our emotional and social wellbeing as it is for our health. Holistic doctors consider getting the right amount of nutritionally balanced food to be 'preventive medicine.' The time we take now to ensure proper diet can be considered an investment in our future well-being.

Over the last hundred years we have seen tremendous progress in kitchen design. Hot and cold running water are now readily available, stoves and ovens that are heated with gas or electricity instead of wood, and mechanical refrigerators have replaced the old-fashioned ice boxes (a cabinet with a block of ice inside to keep things relatively cool).

With these modern amenities, home food storage and preparation meant we had access to more variety of food for longer. This obvious benefit soon meant the sink, stove, and refrigerator became must haves for a modern kitchen, and designers quickly developed the kitchen triangle to reflect the relationship between the three key elements available to homeowners.

Since then, the triangle between the stove, sink, and refrigerator has been the gold standard of kitchen design in any space large enough to accommodate it. Tighter kitchens typically utilize the galley or line kitchen, but the triangle is considered a more versatile and pleasant space for most residential settings.

Surprisingly our kitchen plans and layouts have stayed the same even as our knowledge of nutrition and food preparation has increased, and with it our tools and appliances. The triangle has served us well since the 1950s, and now it is time to build on that. *Conscious Home Design* includes two additional elements — juicing and growing/sprouting stations to create a five-point kitchen.

Doctors, nutritionists, athletes, and health enthusiasts all know the value of increasing their daily intake of fresh fruits and vegetables. We all need to get them into our bodies for good health, good attitude, good mood and good blood sugar and energy levels. These days, most nutrition-conscious people are taking at least one fresh juice or blended energy beverage each day, either as a meal in itself or a supplement to regular meals. Whether they're using a juice extractor or blender (or both), the point is to get fast, easy-to-assimilate energy and nutrition.

Equally essential to juicing is our supply of fresh produce. We want to have access to quality greens with which to make juice and meals. Many options are available to grow sprouts, herbs, and greens right in the home. From a simple sunny window to a green garden wall, options are available for different needs and lifestyles. A few sprouting trays or jars in a sunny window shelf keeps a handful or two of fresh delights coming each day.

There is something about growing your own food, even if it's just a few token plants, that is rewarding and satisfying. Even a tiny step in this direction gives a feeling of self-reliance and security.

When we cultivate greens in our kitchen we receive enjoyment in the form of flavor, nutrition, increased air quality, and the feelings of satisfaction that come from our connection with the rhythm and cycle of nature. This enhances our overall quality of life, health, and sense of fulfillment.

So in the old style kitchens we have the traditional triad. We've now expanded on that to include a sprouting and growing space and a juicing/blending/extracting space. We now can have plenty of fresh fruits and vegetables as part of our regular lifestyle to help satisfy our nutritional needs. This new design serves us even better than the old architecture from the past, and new homes that aren't designed with this awareness.

The reason we consider breakfast the most important meal of the day is because we want to fuel up to get our minds and bodies energized for success each morning. Though we may hold a "good breakfast habit" ideal, we may not always make choices that reflect it. We have busy lives and so we look for ways to simplify. We may just grab a snack bar and a caffeinated drink to take in the car to fuel us through our rush.

This is one of those things that's going to have a cumulative effect over the long term, though. We may be fine today with a coffee and a bagel for breakfast, but a prolonged high calorie/low nutrition start to our day is likely to have a deleterious effect on our overall health and well-being.

Let's use *Conscious Home Design* to help us take a few extra minutes in the morning to prepare something with life energy and nutrition for breakfast, like a green juice or smoothie. If you want to have some caffeinated tea or coffee, go ahead and have that too, but let's make sure you're getting your micronutrients and chlorophyll to include some natural vitality as well, yes?

A simple but powerful design choice we can make to support the "good breakfast habit" is to place the kitchen in the southeast corner of the home. This works in our favor for two reasons — first, we utilize the sunny window effect.

If our kitchen is flooded with morning sun it makes it more inviting, and gives us a little invitation to spend ten minutes making a fruity green juice for ourselves (and our loved ones) and get some nutrition into us before we start our busy and productive day.

Second, that southern exposure makes our kitchens become a little greenhouse where sprouts and herbs grow more quickly, thereby keeping us supplied for juicing, snacking, and salad ingredients. Keeping produce hidden away in the bottom drawer of the refrigerator is not as powerful a reminder to eat our veggies compared to seeing a lush garden growing right over our counter in full view every time we enter the kitchen.

Other essentials to designing kitchens that are excellent spaces for food preparation include lighting, and proximity of counters and appliances to maximize flow and ease of cleaning. The specifics of these and other things should be explored with your architect when planning your kitchen.

Finally, as we covered in the Rule of Sevens, we want to verify the source and quality of water in our homes. Taking the necessary steps to ensure we give ourselves great quality water will help us maintain proper hydration. Drinking plenty of good quality water and having a home water purification system, if needed, are essential aspects of *Conscious Home Design*.

A fun feature we can include to encourage water intake is to add a counter-mounted drinking faucet at the sink. It doesn't cost a lot, but adds novelty and convenience to the home. This neat feature makes it easy for kids and fun-loving adults to drink more water, and it also means fewer cups to wash — saving work, reducing clutter, and enhancing health and enjoyment.

Chapter 6

Rest and Recharge - Bedroom Design for Deep Sleep and Passionate Intimacy

Go to bed happy, wake up refreshed

Bedchamber. Evening Quarters. Boudoir. Whatever we call our bedroom, its purpose is the same: to provide a safe, quiet, place where you can rest, recharge, and rejuvenate. The bedroom has to provide a place for us to get quality sleep so we are better prepared to go about our daily lives.

Bedrooms must also provide a place for intimacy and vulnerability. Just as it is important to our success to be ready to meet daily life with head up and eyes open, it is equally essential that we unwind, let our hair down, and shed any armor. The bedroom is a place we can be completely ourselves, unscripted, and unashamed — naked — both physically and emotionally.

The first purpose of the bedroom has to do with meeting our basic physiological and security needs. The second purpose provides for our higher psychological needs of belonging and esteem. Being naked and vulnerable is about acceptance and trust. Even if we don't share our bedroom with anyone, trust and acceptance begin with ourselves. From this place, we can then give to others in whatever ways we choose, inside and outside of the home.

How does *Conscious Home Design* result in a bedroom design that meets all our needs effectively? When it comes to bedrooms, most people focus on surface materials and colors, textures, and fabrics. These elements definitely help us settle in and feel cozy. These surface materials and furnishings are just the flesh though. Underneath the surface we must align the fundamentals — the "bones," so to speak.

The fundamentals of a space: light, sound, air quality, and orientation, are elements of architecture. Paint color and fabric texture are decoration. We build one upon the other. If the foundational structure isn't right, putting fancy silk dressing on it is nice, but can't overcome the flaws in design. There's no substitute for good structure, and so we start by designing the bedroom environment to be a quiet, private space with fresh air and proper lighting.

For starters, a consciously designed home uses walls, windows, and doors that are well insulated to create a buffer from sound. We don't need to make our bedrooms absolutely soundproof, but a reduced sound transference is desirable to help us rest.

This also has the added benefit of increased privacy so we can have confidential discussions without being overheard, or sexual connection without feeling required to tone it down.

Fresh air is another element of *Conscious Home Design*. When we sleep, our breathing is typically shallower than when we are up and about. Our lungs are further constricted by certain sleep positions. Because of lowered air intake, it is helpful if it is fresh and oxygen-rich. Sleeping in a stuffy room with stale air makes us likely to wake up feeling groggy and less refreshed.

Trivia: The word "window" is an English adaption of the old Norse word "vindauga" which literally translates to "wind eye." Before glass had been invented, people realized that without ventilation air stagnates and humidity can build up and grow mold and mildew. By cutting holes, or "wind eyes" to allow breezes to come through, they made homes and life instantly better. Of course sunlight also came in to brighten the space and ultraviolet rays further purified the air. Though we now fill these holes with panes of glass, we still use the old reference to the wind in recognition perhaps of the importance of fresh air.

Conscious Home Design also means we look carefully at how we orient our rooms and windows to receive natural light. It means we consider our natural circadian rhythms when designing, because light affects our bodies. For example, doctors have discovered that morning sunlight is beneficial in alleviating the symptoms of people suffering from manic depression. Having a bedroom on the west side of the house means not receiving that early morning sunshine.

This doesn't appear to be a problem for healthy people, but clearly the timing of light we receive is something to which the body and mind responds. We evolved to live in concert with the annual seasons of the sun and monthly cycles of the moon and the resulting fluctuations of light. It makes biological sense that we take this into consideration when we design our homes.

Conscious Home Design also means supporting your sense of safety and privacy. Imagine you were required to spend a night out across town on the sidewalk in front of a stranger's home. A guard stands nearby so you don't have to worry about crime of any kind, but still, take a moment and imagine how that feels. Even if you have the best bedding and blankets, there is a feeling of exposure, and you probably wouldn't get the best rest.

Now imagine the same scenario but this time you're sleeping on the sidewalk in front of your own home. This probably feels better, but still exposed. On the third night, you are allowed to sleep inside your home, but on the floor right inside the front door. The added privacy and security would allow most people to get a better night of rest, but it would still be hard to fully relax and settle in. Most people prefer the added layer of another door to a room deeper inside the house.

Conscious Home Design goes a step further than simply a room with a door. It means creating a layout that adds to your peace and comfort. Just because you are inside a bedroom doesn't mean that's the most secure and private you can feel. The orientation of the bed in relationship to doors and windows can have a subtle but marked effect on how deeply we let go and allow ourselves to sleep. Along with sound reduction, these exposure points subtly influence and can reduce or increase our sense of privacy and the quality of our sleep.

Getting proper rest is *essential* to our health and wellbeing. When our sleep quality goes up, we need less of it, and we are more effective in our daily activities. When we don't get good, regular sleep, we don't perform as well, our work suffers, our interactions with others are less positive, our immune systems decline and our mental faculties become compromised.

The brain needs sleep to grow and repair neural networks. Just as our muscles and fibers need time to rest and recover, so do our brain tissues. Young and old, our minds need time to rest! Sound, light, circadian rhythms, electromagnetic frequencies (EMFs) and experiencing the full range of sleep cycles (including REM and Deep Sleep) all factor into how refreshed we feel upon waking. We all know from experience that a good night's rest changes our day. We might also notice that several days and weeks of consecutive good sleep compounds to give us life changing strength and ability. With *Conscious Home Design* we create the conditions for optimal, life-enhancing sleep.

Finally, your romantic life can flourish in a well designed space. The bedroom provides an opportunity to connect at a more personal level with our partner. It's where we transition to becoming our most vulnerable — personally and physically. It's where we have private time, connect, and feel the freedom to have a unique flavor of relationship to which no other family members are privy. As we undress both literally and figuratively, having a safe space for sleeping and intimacy is an essential part of human life.

Chapter 7

Bathing

Every Day is a Spa Day

Trivia: Do you know why hot water is always on the left and cold on the right? This standard comes from the evolution of plumbing. In generations past, people had to leave their homes to fetch water for cooking and cleaning. When technology and industry made pipes available at a reasonable cost, it wasn't long before we ran water pipes into the house. Of course all we had at that time was unheated water, and since most people are right handed, we installed the water handle on the right of the sink basin. Later, when technology further developed and allowed for hot water in our buildings, we placed that handle on the left where there was room. To this day, building codes require that we maintain this convention. Even if a faucet has a single handle, when turned or pushed to the left we get hot water, and cold on the right.

Earlier, in the first chapter, we covered how we can simply and creatively build opportunities for all three types of relationship in the bathroom. In the past, bathrooms were seen as simply serving a utilitarian function, a basic mundane space holding rank just above the basement or storage closet. In fact, toilets were called *water closets* by architects in years past. This utilitarian approach leaves a great opportunity overlooked.

The bathroom is a place where we care for our bodies, where we refresh and energize our skin, and get the blood circulating. When our body feels fresh, our mind and spirit are uplifted as well. This grooming, bathing, and self-care releases oxytocin along with other hormones, increasing feelings of connection and bonding, and boosts our feelings of peace, happiness, and enthusiasm.

Having a bright bathroom with natural light, fresh air, and qualities of vitality and energy really supports us in starting each day at our best. As we covered in the bedroom chapter, when we sleep, our breathing is shallower. When we wake and rise we naturally take deeper breaths to fill our lungs and oxygenate our body. The morning air we breathe plays a direct role in how invigorated we feel, and many of our first morning breaths are in the bathroom.

When we rethink the full purpose of bathrooms and see the potential they have to support us, we stop designing them like mundane utilitarian rooms and more like a kind of 'rejuvenation sanctuary'. Bathrooms deserve careful and thoughtful planning.

In addition to being a place to groom, wash, and refresh, bathrooms include a toilet where we relieve our bladders and bowels. There is a holistic, even symbiotic relationship between the kitchen and bathroom. Just as getting proper nutrients into the body is part of conscious living, getting waste and unneeded elements out is equally essential. Though few people talk about it, the deeper fact of the matter is that we need to take care of our elimination needs. Without proper elimination, we slowly build up toxins in the system which lead to long-term health problems including fatigue, mental sluggishness, and premature aging.

In *Conscious Home Design* we create a bathroom space where a person can relax and let go to fully release waste the body no longer needs. A bathroom that is comfortable and inviting, and meets privacy needs creates a sense of ease that is helpful to both our physical bodies and our mental attitude and outlook.

Have you ever noticed that constipated people are grumpier? This is especially evident in children and the elderly. They seem particularly responsive, but if we pause to notice, people of any age feel a little lift of happiness after visiting the toilet, and come out of the bathroom with an extra spring in their step, sometimes even singing, humming, or smiling. There is a feeling of lightness after releasing what is no longer needed. When the body feels good, the mind is naturally cheerful. When we feel cheerful, we have more courage and confidence.

Near the bathroom is an ideal place for a laundry room. An acquaintance of mine got married and she and her husband decided to have a nice million dollar home built for them. After they moved in they had their first child, and she soon became pregnant with child number two. During this time she was lamenting that the laundry room was in the basement of her two-story home.

There she was, pregnant, with a little toddler running around creating a lot of dirty clothes that she had to tote up and down two flights of stairs. Add to that the challenge of keeping her eye on a very active toddler and something as basic as laundry was adding unnecessary struggle to her day. She had this extra work because her architect was thinking of laundry as a utility feature that belongs in a basement with the furnace and plumbing instead of being sensitive to the way people move through space.

When we get dressed and undressed we are typically in the bedroom/closet/bathroom area so it makes sense to have the laundry room right there where our clothes are shed, donned, and stored. It makes sense from a basic ease-of-functionality perspective. Additionally, when someone is sick, injured, aged, or infirm, proximity to laundry appliances becomes even more important.

Of course using the stairs on laundry days is good exercise, but if someone is relying on an occasional use of stairs on laundry day to get their exercise quota in, then we really need to look for ways to build a joyful home that includes ample opportunity to move the body in other ways. We'll cover this more in the movement chapter. So let's go ahead and make doing laundry as efficient and easy as possible and focus on moving our bodies by doing something we really enjoy doing, like dancing or martial arts or yoga or cycling, etc.

Chapter 8

Reception - Creating an Entry Hall that Welcomes You Home

Welcome Home!

Trivia: Have you noticed that the front doors on most homes swing inwards? This is because we can get a better seal and protect the edges of the door by closing it against a strip around the frame. This prevents water and wind from seeping in around the edges. Conversely, doors in public commercial spaces swing out. Though it is not as weather tight, we do this for safety reasons. In a public building with many occupants it is easier to exit quickly if there is need to evacuate. In public buildings, doors open in the direction of travel for people *leaving* the building. In our homes, we design doors for security and energy efficiency. And depending on your design preferences, we can also make them fun, bright, creative, elegant, and welcoming.

Picture this: You're on your way to the front door, arms full of gear, groceries, whatever, and your cell phone is ringing while you fumble with the lock. You manage to get inside without dropping anything, but you have to make a mad dash to the toilet because you've been holding your water for the last 35 minutes because the traffic was terrible. Now you're inside and dump everything and kick off your shoes and get to that bathroom...

Whew, ok, so now back to the entry area to take care of things. Was there a good drop zone for those grocery bags or are they on the floor now? Are you able to stow your shoes and coat neatly, or are there already too many shoes and coats cluttering up the place? And what did you do with the keys? Are they in your pocket, or still in the door lock, or did you carry them with you and then accidentally leave them in the bathroom?

It was hectic out there today; you've been out in the rush and bustle of the world and now you land on your doorstep and need to transition from there to the sanctity of your home. The entry is where we move and decompress from the public space of the outside world to the personal private space our home.

This transition space for our arrival and departure is inherently a high friction zone. Just as the wheels of an airplane screech and smoke as they synchronize their rotation to the ground as the plane touches down, so too, in a way, do we have a moment of adjustment when we move from one zone to another.

You've probably experienced coming home with too much stress of the day on your shoulders, only to have that burden cause strife and friction with your loved ones. A good transition space can help us downshift and leave more of that tension behind, take a deep breath and relax into our home. With *Conscious Home Design* we create a well-planned entry, a buffer zone that helps us decompress and leave the bustle and hustle of life at the entry door so we can step into a relaxing, rejuvenating sanctuary: our home.

The space in our home has a different feel than outside. The difference between public and private is distinct. If you just walk right into the living room or other part of the house right off the street it's very abrupt. The foyer allows us a space to shed some of the "armor" we wear in the street. It is our buffer between private and public areas, or what architects (sometimes exaggeratingly) refer to as "sacred and profane" spaces.

When we enter our home, we need a practical space with closets and cubbies for our gear and outerwear, and counterspace for groceries, mail, and shopping bags to sit while we put our boots and jackets away. Having this decompression chamber and storage space is essential to preserving harmony in the home. Boots, coats, and outside necessities need to be checked at the door so they don't spill into our living environment.

When the foyer has proper space to hang our hats, umbrellas, sunglasses, keys and other essentials then we know where they are when we need them the next time we leave. This organization saves time and worry. We design so we aren't rushing around looking for some misplaced item and leaving home stressed and late, which can spiral into traffic frustrations and add to the sense of frenzy.

Then when we arrive at work or wherever we are going, perhaps we have lost some of the poise and grace we had carried before the rush began. This can impact and affect our day, our interactions with others, and our success.

The entry space is also designed to be a statement, a testimony to our style and values. We can create it to be stately and formal, joyful and invigorating, calming and serene, or rustic and comfortable. It is where we welcome ourselves and our guests home and begin to tell the story of our lives and family.

We can personalize an entry after we have made sure it addresses our practical needs by creating a focal point around something we value and love. We can place one to see as we enter and transition to the inside sanctity we enjoy, and one as we exit to give us a little send-off encouraging us to be our best and carry that with us into the outside world. These focal points can be a piece of art or sculpture, a statue, mirror, fountain, or photo collage. What story do we want to tell, what values do we want to remind ourselves and our guests of as we come and go from our home?

The foyer is one of the most overlooked spaces in residential architecture, but because it is one of the highest friction zones in the home, we gain valuable efficiency by organizing this critical transition space. After the house has done its job of nourishing and rejuvenating us, the foyer's job is to give us that goodbye kiss and cheerful send-off that greases our tracks and puts a little extra wind in our sails. It's our jumping off point, where we gear up and head out into the great wild blue yonder.

A well-designed launch pad helps us to leave our homes feeling awake and ready, happy and optimistic, ready to face the day. When we go forth into the world we want to look and feel our best, and put our best foot forward. A Consciously Designed foyer sends us off with a smile, and welcomes us home with open arms. It blesses us and our guests whether we are going or coming.

Chapter 9

Outer Development - Physical Movement Space

Design that Encourages Body Movement for Fitness and Fun

Where do you fall on the exercise spectrum? Are you an avid health and fitness enthusiast who exercises daily or are you someone whose activity level is limited to walking to and from the car on the way to work? Do you struggle to get yourself to exercise or is it something you love to do and find it easy to prioritize?

You can be one or the other, or somewhere in between, but the bottom line is that people who move their bodies in some way tend to be healthier and happier. Is there a particular physical activity that you love to do? What if we could find a way for you to do more of it? Let's look at how we can use *Conscious Home Design* to support you in being physically active at a level that works for you.

If you're a fitness enthusiast, *Conscious Home Design* will do three key things for you: a) it will create opportunity for you to log in more exercise time, b) keep your goals front and center to encourage you to reach new levels, and c) celebrate the achievements and milestones you've already gained from your efforts.

If you are someone who is aware of the benefits of exercise, but have not been able to incorporate it into your routine, *Conscious Home Design* will help you get moving in a way that is easy and fun for you. We can design ways to bring movement into your life that doesn't feel like a chore or drudgery, and we can do it without stealing all of your precious time.

We start by looking for physical activities that are inherently appealing and fun for you, such as dance or yoga or fencing or martial arts rather than working out with machines and weights. We want to find something that is *intrinsically* interesting to you for its own sake, not just because it has a specific fitness benefit. This will help remove some of the resistance to exercise, and at the same time increase the feeling of fun and happiness.

Next, we are going to use design to support us in engaging in that activity. I've seen a lot of people throw a treadmill and a weight bench in the garage, or fix up the basement to make a home gym. This sounds like a good idea at first, a natural use of space, but unless you are on the far end of the enthusiast spectrum these strategies are destined for failure sooner or later.

A basement gym is certainly better than not having a workout space at all, but the reality is that basements have notoriously poor light and air quality; they're not very inviting. Unless you really love to exercise and are highly motivated, you'll need to use extra willpower to make yourself go down there. If you're tight on time, short on sleep, or tired from a tough day the last thing you probably want to do is go into the "torture dungeon" and make yourself sweat.

Sure, an uninspiring environment that sits out of sight are small hiccups that we can overcome when we're fully rested, not pressed for time, and feeling on top of our game. But what if you're tight on time and only have ten minutes instead of twenty? It hardly seems worth it to go down there. Not only is it not a beautiful environment beckoning you to come enjoy yourself, it's also easy to avoid and skip for the day. Even if we created a basement space to do something you really enjoy, like dancing or yoga, it still has the same inherent problems and challenges of being a space meant for storage, and we can use conscious design to do better than that.

Once when I was visiting my sister I inquired about the things she had set on the stairs by the door — I thought they were a tripping hazard. She informed me they were important items she wanted to remember to take with her and by placing them in the line of traffic she was essentially forcing herself to succeed.

We can utilize this strategy to encourage us to perform activities we may struggle to accomplish. When we are trying to create and strengthen an exercise habit, we can locate this activity space directly in the line of circulation so that we go right by (or through) the space every day. By placing our exercise space in the path of least resistance- on the way from the bedroom to the kitchen for example, we give ourselves greater chance of success.

In addition to the circulation tactic, we can further support our success by utilizing the Sunny Window Effect. Now, not only have we selected an activity that we enjoy and made it easy to access, we also have a dedicated zone for it that is inviting. You only have to take a few steps and voilà, you are right where you want to be — in a cheerful, inviting, sunny place that welcomes you in. So rather than relying on will power alone to get your body moving, let's build your success right into the design of your home.

What if your favorite activities are outdoor sports and recreation, or you're a person who is a real fitness enthusiast who heads to the gym six days a week? Do you still need to create a physical activity space in your home?

It might seem impossible if your favorite way to move is an outdoor team sport like playing baseball in a local league. It might be infeasible to install a batting cage in your home. But we can definitely encourage this aspect of your life with *Conscious Home Design*. For example, rather than keeping a gear bag hidden in the garage or trunk of the car, let's look for a way to store these or other favorite items in a way that will be seen every day.

Is there a way to showcase your sporting equipment that is tasteful and appealing, to create a "wall of sports" in your home? Can we also display photos of you and/or your teammates or heroes and any awards, medals, and trophies you've received?

Whether you enjoy a team sport or a solo sport like skiing, kayaking, or cycling, we can explore ways to store and display your equipment so that it stays top of mind, easy to access, and celebrates activities you are passionate about.

Finally, let's take into consideration the natural ebb and flow and challenges of life in our design strategies. Some sports are seasonal. Even during the right season, some can't be done in inclement weather. Sometimes we are pressed for time, and sometimes we are having a low-energy day for whatever reason. Having a physical activity space built into our home allows us to stay active regardless of all these factors.

When the weather is off we can still move. When we don't have enough time to make the commute to the gym we can still move. When we are feeling low and don't want to get out and work hard, we can stay home and stretch or do some low-key movement that suits us. Let's also keep in mind that we change. Our interests or abilities may evolve and transitioning from one activity to another can be smoother with a built-in movement space at home.

When we create a movement space in our home, we always have the opportunity to benefit regardless of the weather, our age, health, interest or ability. The magic of movement is that we always feel better after doing it but sometimes it's tough to overcome the initial inertia. By building space for an activity we love in our home — a yoga room, or exercise room — or equipment storage area where we neatly, sleekly and keenly display our favorite bike, skis, surf/snowboard, etc. then we have every possible encouragement from our environment to get healthful, enjoyable activity into our day.

Chapter 10

Inner Development - Tuning in and Cultivating Wisdom and Peace

As within, so without...

When we are feeling strong, confident, and centered we can walk through the storms of life with peace and poise. Conversely, when we are agitated and off kilter, then even a perfect sunny day does little to lift our spirits. Therefore, carrying a sense of harmony within you is the ultimate priority. *Conscious Home Design* places a tremendous value on dedicating space in your home for your inner development. As we know, when we create *space* for our activities, it becomes easier for us to create the *time* to do them.

We're working right at the top of the pyramid of needs now for personal development, self-actualization, and transcendence. Your home is your castle and your home is also your temple. Our growth curve doesn't end after college or whatever school we completed. Even if it did, the educational system doesn't teach us everything we need to know to have a full life. We are lifelong learners and our development unfolds over time. The process happens naturally, but we can also accelerate it with active engagement, and by using conscious design.

Our inner life includes our mental, emotional, and spiritual facets. When any one of these aspects is troubled, it can adversely affect the others, and consequently disrupt or limit our external success. To our benefit though, a strong, clear state in any one of them will also strengthen the others. There is a symbiotic relationship. When we are strong and clear in all three areas of our inner life, then a powerful synergy occurs and we are virtually unstoppable.

How can we use architecture to help ourselves experience more of that alignment? Inner development space shows up in different ways for different people. Some people are more intellectual, others are devoutly spiritual. My grandfather, for example, was of a predominantly intellectual disposition. A Harvard graduate, he was a professor of economics at Williams, and the President of Colgate University. He spoke five languages and completed the New York Times crossword puzzle in pen.

Because of his Scientific Rationalist perspective, his inner development space was his study. Along with his big wooden desk, filing cabinet for important papers, and wall to wall, floor-to-ceiling bookshelves, he had a chair and a couch upon which to read and contemplate (and take an afternoon nap).

He also had art, carvings, and mementos from around the world in his study — souvenirs from his cultural adventures and periodic consulting work abroad. All this served to strengthen his focus and inquisitiveness, and he kept his mind sharp and alert into his 90s.

For someone with strong spiritual inclination, a prayer and meditation room will support their inner life. I read about a married couple who were of differing opinions: The husband had a cold indifference to spiritual things, while his wife was very devotional and possessed a deep faith in the existence of a universal and loving, intelligent God.

She had a tiny room to which she would go and pray to feel closer to her Creator, but she was sad that she was alone in her practice. Through a series of events, however, her husband had a direct and profound personal experience that caused him to share in his wife's conviction of the existence of a supreme and benevolent God.

After his epiphany, he realized that cultivating a personal connection with God was a high priority for himself, as well. So they moved their bed into a smaller room so that they could rededicate their larger bedroom as a meditation and prayer space. For him, giving the larger room to their devotional practice was a way to demonstrate priority and importance. This physical act affirmed his inner belief and supported his external practice.

Of course, this doesn't mean that we design our spaces by size in descending order according to the importance of the activity they support. As an architect, I believe that spaces should be sized properly to serve their function.

Too big is wasteful and too small limits the room's ability to accommodate its intended purpose. *The example of the couple simply shows that when we create space for something, we give it value — we are affirming the importance of that part of our lives.*

Continuing on the subject of scale, size really does matter in home design. Cathedral ceilings and panoramic windows do wonders to give us a feeling of expansion, inspiring a greater sense of possibility and potential. On the other hand, Albert Einstein said he preferred small, tight spaces with low ceilings for doing his studying and work. Concentrating the mind is similar to how a magnifying glass works; by capturing an area of sunlight and focusing it into a single, targeted beam. The directed energy we apply from concentration gives us the ability to burn up obstacles and pave the way to our success.

Sometimes our activities call for expansion, other times they call for concentration. If we have something that we are studying, or a project we're working on that requires longer periods of sustained thought, we can actually build an environment for ourselves that is free of clutter and distraction to help us concentrate. Just entering a room like that can help us attain a state of focused attention. Whether you are concentrating on things of the mind or things of the spirit, *Conscious Home Design* can support your efforts.

To further support mindfulness and/or spirituality we can also create opportunity throughout a home to keep our values top of mind as we go through our day. In addition to having a room solely dedicated to personal growth and self-actualization, we can also have a little spot in other rooms in the house, such as an image or altar, an inspirational phrase or affirmation. In this way we use design to integrate our inner strengths and values with all our other activities.

Life is more than a simple series of separate activities. Though we achieve better results when we focus on one activity at a time, our inner work is about carrying that skill and concentration into everything we do. What we gain through study, mindfulness, and meditation, we want to carry with us into daily life — whether we're exercising, cooking, cleaning, working, or anything else. This inner balance is the thread that weaves all our activities together into the tapestry of our life.

So we set up reminders in our lives throughout our homes to help us stay on course. We create a loving and supportive environment that aids us in realizing our greatest goals and aspirations, bringing us steadily toward self-actualization. We use *Conscious Home Design* to build it into your home.

Chapter 11

From the Inside Out - Express Yourself! Making Room for Creativity

Fanning the Creative Spark

How does creativity show up in your life? What kinds of creative things do you like to do? How about the people who are close to you? If you were going to build creative space into your home, what would that be like for everyone? Would one room work to accommodate everyone, or would you want to have separate spaces for some activities?

We are all inherently creative. We can express it through our work, our wardrobe, our cooking, and the more "traditional" forms like painting, writing, sculpture, music or dance. Whether your creative efforts are visual, auditory, literary, or performance-based, creative expression is one of our highest needs, part of our self-actualization as represented at the top section of the pyramid.

I once attended a concert in the front parlor of a family's home. This was a musical clan; everyone in the family had been a professional musician for *seven* generations! They lived together, practiced together, and performed together. Their home had been in their family for hundreds of years and *of course* they had a music room. This situation is rare obviously. More often than not, individual family members have different and varied interests, some of which may not blend so well. Most families wouldn't want to put a drum set in the living room, whereas a piano occupies about the same amount of floor area, and is much more commonly accepted as living room material.

You might be surprised to learn how relatively simple it actually is to provide architectural details that substantially dampen the sound transference from one room to the next. When I worked on a project for a government security contractor that didn't want conversations to be overheard from one office to the next, I dug deep into various ways to answer that challenge as affordably as possible. I have also used this knowledge to create more privacy between guest rooms in meditation retreat centers, so visitors experience less distraction.

This technology is certainly available for your home, should you find the need to create more separation from one room to another. A sound barrier can be used in a bedroom to encourage deep sleep, or a creative room that might be loud enough to disturb others who are concentrating on homework, listening to music, watching a show, or just relaxing. So if someone really wants those drums, it is possible to make room for that without requiring the rest of the family (or neighbors) to be musicians, too.

At the root of it, creativity is how we take that which is inside of us and make it visible on the outside. It is an essential part of being alive, of being human. *Conscious Home Design* is about noticing the natural creative abilities in each person, and supporting, encouraging, and nurturing those talents through architecture. We can have all of our physical needs met, but if we don't find some form of creative expression we will feel like something is missing. Creating is as much about ourselves as it is for the people we create for. Remember the story from the first chapter? Sometimes we create for others, sometimes we create for ourselves.

Most homes simply don't provide dedicated space for creative practice. A large, beautiful home in a safe neighborhood with all the modern amenities can still feel stifling if it doesn't effectively nurture our creative sides. By building creativity into our lives, we kindle zest and enthusiasm. We are all born with some form of passion, and finding a way to hold onto it and express it in adulthood makes life rich and rewarding.

There is another reason to encourage individual creativity in the home: harmony. In the living and dining areas, we covered the subject of coming together as a family, and creating a home that supports the family as a whole. It is equally essential to create space for individual family members to explore life in their own personal way. Each person is an individual with their own goals and personalities. Their styles and unique qualities are part of the collage. Happier individuals are going to have happier interactions with others. When each person's individual needs are met there is much more likelihood that when the family comes together there will be more peace, harmony, and enjoyment.

Is a separate, dedicated room always necessary? What if your creative ventures exist outside of the home at a job, studio, or in the backyard garden? What if you consider your kitchen to be where you find creative expression via the food you prepare?

Creativity comes in many forms; some people choose creative expression in very integrated, practical ways, such as organizing or planning. Other types of creativity may fall more under the category of "art" such as painting or sculpting, which typically have more spatial requirements. Because people express creativity in multiple ways, for the purpose of personal fulfillment and self-actualization we can't say one is better than another — it's a subjective experience.

In *Conscious Home Design* we look at the creative interests of everyone in the household — maybe one person's creative expression doesn't need a dedicated space but another's activity does. To accommodate everyone's creativity, sometimes separate spaces are needed, and sometimes multiple creative projects can be artfully blended and happen in the same space. As with the living room, sometimes a creative space can accommodate group activity where multiple people are doing the same activity together in *active* together time, and other times people can be doing their own individual activities in the same space in *passive* together time.

Finally, we can look to an individual's past — was there something you really loved doing when you were growing up, or before you had a busy career or family responsibilities that absorbed your time? When we build a dedicated space into a home, we create opportunity to bring those activities back into our lives. If you don't have anything from your past to resurrect or rekindle, you can decide if there is something new you would like to try. Since it is never too late to start (or restart) something where creative expression is concerned, I recommend that a dedicated room or area for creative activity be incorporated into every home to allow people to grow, to thrive, and explore new things.

CONSCIOUS HOME DESIGN

for Happiness, Health, and Relationship Success

Chapter 12

Bringing it all Together

Going From Big Picture to Tiny Details

We have covered the big picture concepts of the Hierarchy of Human Needs, the Rule of Sevens, the Butterfly Effect, the Three Types of Relationship, and the Sunny Window Effect. We also went through the Nine Essential Spaces one at a time to illustrate how they each play a role in *Conscious Home Design*, and the relationship between the big picture concepts and these spaces. We also explored different levels of privacy these activities have — some spaces require connection, others require more separation.

All this is to highlight the major factors we should account for when designing homes for us to live our fullest, best lives. Though this list is far-reaching and comprehensive compared to conventional home design, it is only an outline. *Conscious Home Design* is about taking these pieces, discovering how they can be uniquely applied and arranged so that the whole house flows for the homeowner. This is the art of design — reducing friction, and increasing ease of use. I like to call this "grace."

The design of your home will be uniquely suited to you. It can't be shown in a book. There are little details though that we can cover here that will help anyone create grace in their home. There are many of course, some of which were given in the individual sections, like a drinking fountain in the kitchen. In this section, let's focus on three that have daily, direct impact: Flooring, Faucets, and Door Handles. These may not seem exciting at first glance, but they are worth discovering for your comfort and enjoyment.

What about flooring? What your feet touch, your whole body feels. Some people like wood and others like tile. Some think polished concrete is cool and some prefer the warmth and cushion of carpet. Carpet is ideal for some areas because it's softer and it also dampens sound, reducing echo and increasing a sense of intimacy.

Hard surfaces are generally easier to keep clean, but are less forgiving on feet, joints, and dropped objects. My grandmother had a wall to wall, low-pile carpet and pad in her kitchen! She spent many hours of her day lovingly preparing food for herself, her husband, and their five children. She found the ease on her feet and fewer incidents of broken jars and dishes far outweighed the hassle of food spills. It also made the kitchen feel cozier — kitchens are prone to echo and this reflected noise is particularly exaggerated when using blenders, processors, and other equipment.

I personally am a lover of smoothies and blends. I think it's a great way to quickly make a nutritious and tasty snack or drink, and liquifying foods makes them easier to digest so the body can absorb more nutrients. But blenders are loud. One of the items in my architect's tool kit however, is a sound meter. So I went to work to see what I could do to dampen the noise from my blender. I tried many things, from shields, to wrapping, to operating it in its own little box. What I discovered, happily, was that one of the easiest and simplest solutions to use was also the most effective. I found that placing the blender on a 12x12 inch piece of cork (which can typically be picked up as a free or low-cost sample from a flooring store) reduced the sound level by 10 decibels.

This is one of the many reasons why cork flooring is such a great product. It is quiet, it is softer than wood but easier to clean than carpet, and it is a renewable resource. Cork is actually the bark from a species of oak tree. The outer layer of bark is carefully removed, leaving the tree unharmed and able to grow a new "coat" in the same way we get wool from sheep.

Speaking of sheep, if carpet is something you really want in your home, wool is the gold standard. Some carpet salesmen will try very hard to convince you that synthetic fibers impregnated with stain guard, flame retardant, moisture blockers and mildew inhibitors are the product of choice. Maybe this is because the chemical companies that make those products push them very hard to their distributors and sales force, and that in turn trickles down to the consumer. There may be some situations where these synthetics are preferable, but I try to avoid using them in a home.

What is challenging about synthetic carpet is that the odor can last for many months after installation and ruin indoor air quality. They also don't feel as nice on the skin, so if you or the kids like to play on the carpet, that's a friction point. Synthetics also generate static electricity more readily than wool, particularly in the heating season. Have you ever walked across a carpet and received an electric shock when you reached for the doorknob? This is largely a function of humidity, so wool does not completely eliminate it, but it is less prone than synthetics because of the way the fiber molecules hold onto their electrons. This is a little irritation we can minimize with *Conscious Home Design*.

We want to pay attention to air quality, and humidity levels, and careful selection of the carpet material. If you have allergies or irritation to wool in particular, other natural fibers like silk or jute are used in floor coverings and generally offgas less, and create less static electricity than synthetics. So put something natural under your feet and breathe a sigh of relief and relaxation.

What about faucets? Remember the cold on the right and hot on the left trivia? Sometimes the old-fashioned styles reflect this history and have two levers, one for hot and one for cold. From an ease of use perspective, it's much easier to have a single lever faucet, be it in the bathroom or kitchen or any sink in the house, because it can be operated and adjusted with one hand. You can certainly use a two-handled faucet if that's your preference; however if you can find something in a single-handle faucet that meets your design taste or style then all the better.

Additionally, a single-lever faucet is less likely to drip — fewer parts to maintain. Obviously, dripping faucets aren't very fun. They're wasteful, annoying, and can potentially wear down or discolor the materials of some basins over time. Designers certainly consider it bad Feng Shui. So we carefully choose a quality faucet that has a positive stop so the water shuts off completely, every time. The quality of washer/gasket or valve means a lot. So check the materials, manufacturer, and warranty.

Also, when choosing a quality style that's easy to use and easy to maintain, I highly recommend you visit a showroom before you select any faucet. Faucets are like shoes — there are lots of attractive ones at fair prices online, but how well do they fit? Does it extend far enough into the basin, or are your hands knocking against the back of the sink every time you wash them?

Can you get a pot underneath it, or fill a glass of water when there are dishes in the sink?

Finally, is the handle comfortable to touch? Are the handle edges too thin so it feels a little sharp, or is it too short and hard to reach? The handle has to be easy to operate and also feel right in your hand. You touch it multiple times a day, so why not take a twenty minutes and put your hands on every handle in the showroom and feel which ones are comfortable?

This might seem like a small thing, and it is, but you will see what a difference it makes when you realize you have a faucet you truly love. This ergonomic experience extends to door knobs as well. Doorknobs are something we touch many times every single day, just like faucets, yet typically, we don't think too much about them. It's one of those things we just live with because it's always been that way, it came with the house, we haven't been shown another way to look at it. However, it's definitely worthwhile to spend time shopping for door knobs that suit both your design taste but more importantly your hand comfort.

There are many styles to choose from and the showcase pieces are gorgeous, but think less about how it looks and more about what it feels like to grasp. A lot of handles are very beautiful but are uncomfortable, and when you grab hold it feels wrong, or presses the inside of your hand in an ill-fitting way. Why not make it ergonomic and fit beautifully into your hand? Just like with faucets, you want to visit a showroom or two and get your hands on as many door handles as possible to see how they feel.

Lever handles are typically easier to use than knobs because you don't have to grasp them. Your hands can be full, you can have a box in your arms and you can hit it with part of your hand or even with an elbow to operate it. This is convenient and efficient. It's also helpful for small children that have a hard time reaching, grasping, and pulling all at the same time; and also for the elderly, who may have difficulty with arthritic joints, or anyone with limited mobility or strength issues. Levers or other non-grasping type handles are required on public and commercial doors by the Americans with Disabilities Act (ADA) but in residential design they are also catching on for the same reasons — they're a great choice for a multigenerational home.

Regardless of whether you select knobs or levers or any other type of handle and latch, it should *feel* right. If you don't love your door knobs, this is something you can remedy right now. If you look online for a local design center you can go and physically touch and feel as many door knobs as you want until you find one that you absolutely love. It should feel good in your hand. You want to love the feel of opening and closing doors in your home. It's so easy to change a doorknob, especially an interior one — all you typically need is a screwdriver. It's an easy way to give your hands a little grace, and like well chosen faucet handles, you'll find yourself smiling when you use them. Every little thing we do to reduce friction in the home will have a cumulative effect. Less distraction, less friction, and less "noise." More ease, more enjoyment, and more peace.

Ultimately, this peace helps bring us to the state of transcendence at the top of the pyramid of human needs. Transcendence is that state of being where we have reached our goals, achieved our greatness, expressed ourselves creatively or according to our values and intentions, so the things and circumstances around us hold less importance. We are able to spend more time helping others become *their* best selves. This is why we admire saints and humanitarians so much — they are busy working for the benefit of others, and have transcended their own needs in some way. This isn't denial, or a willful ignoring of their own personal needs — heroes and martyrs do this for a short time, but it is not a sustainable way to live.

Transcendence is about living in an elevated state of mind, and a simplified state of external circumstances. Put another way, it is plain living and high thinking. Maslow added transcendence to the top of the pyramid later in life, after realizing it is a definite and distinct human experience and need.

Henry David Thoreau is a great example of this. When I was in my internship in Boston I worked with an architecture and engineering firm that worked on the Thoreau Institute at Walden Pond in Concord. I was able to walk in the woods around the pond and see the original site where Thoreau built his cabin, and visit a reproduction of it. I have looked many times at my photos of the one-room cabin and how he compartmentalized the space. Inside, he had dedicated zones for sleeping, eating, food preparation, study and creativity. Because the cabin was surrounded by hundreds of acres of woods, he used the outdoors for his exercise, and bathroom, and living room, and alas, he didn't have much of an entry space to his little cabin except a door and a coat hook. Even still, he only spent a short time there as an experiment, and later moved into larger accommodations.

So even in context of a very minimalist lifestyle full of service there are things we can do to support ourselves so that we can do our work better, and with more impact, and for a longer amount of time. Having our needs met helps us be greater, and it helps us help others, and the cycle is complete. *Conscious Home Design* is a way to support people in the places we go to be ourselves, the places we go to be together, and to be alone, to rest, recharge, and celebrate life: our homes.

Our lives are the collective sum total of our actions. The way we move our bodies each day defines and comprises our life. Our homes and architecture guide how we move. Let's build consciously, so that our movements are effectively directed, so that our homes are helpful assets that support our goals and ideals. Look to the horizon; the sky is above, and the earth is below. That is where we build. Your home is literally where heaven and earth meet.

Happy Living!

Talor Stewart, Architect

If you would like to explore these ideas more fully, and how they can be expressed in your own home, be sure to check out the Conscious Home Design Workbook. *It's a great companion to this book and a good next step for those who are interested in working more directly with me on a project.*

www.ConsciousHomeDesign.com

Notes

Notes

Notes